Great Big Animals

COLOSSAL CROCODILES

By Francis MacIntire

Please visit our website, www.garethstevens.com. For a free color catalog of all our high-quality books, call toll free 1-800-542-2595 or fax 1-877-542-2596.

Cataloging-in-Publication Data

Names: MacIntire, Francis.
Title: Colossal crocodiles / Francis MacIntire.
Description: New York : Gareth Stevens Publishing, 2018. | Series: Great big animals | Includes index.
Identifiers: ISBN 9781538208953 (pbk.) | ISBN 9781538208977 (library bound) | ISBN 9781538208960 (6 pack)
Subjects: LCSH: Crocodiles–Juvenile literature.
Classification: LCC QL666.C925 M33 2018 | DDC 597.98'2–dc23

First Edition

Published in 2018 by
Gareth Stevens Publishing
111 East 14th Street, Suite 349
New York, NY 10003

Editor: Kate Mikoley
Designer: Sarah Liddell

Photo credits: Cover, p. 1 Ryan M. Bolton/Shutterstock.com; p. 5 Anton_Ivanov/Shutterstock.com; p. 7 Andaman/Shutterstock.com; p. 9 fritz16/Shutterstock.com; p. 11 BineArnold/Shutterstock.com; p. 13 Firepac/Shutterstock.com; pp. 15, 21 v.schlichting/Shutterstock.com; p. 17 Utopia_88/Shutterstock.com; pp. 19, 24 (tail) coolbiere photograph/Moment/Getty Images; p. 23 Stuart G Porter/Shutterstock.com; p. 24 (lake) Yury Yanshin/Shutterstock.com.

Printed in the United States of America

CPSIA compliance information: Batch #CW18GS: For further information contact Gareth Stevens, New York, New York at 1-800-542-2595.

Contents

Crocodiles are big animals!

Some grow
20 feet long!

They live near water. Many live in rivers and lakes.

Some live in salt water.

They are very heavy.

They move slow on land.

They swim very fast!

They use their tail
to move.

They like to sit
in the sun.
This is called basking.

They eat small animals, such as birds and fish.

Words to Know

lake

tail

Index